# "The World Economy and the Russo-Ukrainian War" Towards a Geo-Economy of Blocks?

Written By: La Petite Fleur Bleue

First published on: Draft2digital “2025”

**Summary :**

# Chapter 1: The World Economy on the Eve of Conflict: A Colossus with Feet of Clay (2020-2022)

**The scars of the COVID-19 pandemic:** Analysis of already strained global supply chains, record public and private debt, and the first post-lockdown inflationary pressures.

**The nascent energy transition:** Tensions on energy markets even before the conflict, with rising demand and insufficient investment in both fossil fuels and renewables.

**Precarious geopolitical balances:** Rising Sino-American tensions and erosion of multilateral institutions.

**Focus on Russia and Ukraine:** The respective weight of the two nations in the world economy before the conflict (breadbaskets, suppliers of energy and critical metals).

# Chapter 2: The Shockwave of 2022: The Triple Shock to Energy, Food, and Finance

**The energy shock:** Soaring gas and oil prices. Analysis of European, particularly German, dependence on Russian gas.

**The food shock:** Blockades of Black Sea ports, soaring prices of cereals and vegetable oils. Impact on global food security, particularly in North Africa and the Middle East.

**The financial shock:** Massive financial sanctions, freezing of Russian central bank assets, collapse of the ruble (initial), and panic on the stock markets.

**Immediate consequence:** The return of double-digit inflation in advanced economies and the specter of stagflation.

# Chapter 3: The Great Energy Reorganization (2023-2025)

**Europe's pivot:** A quantitative analysis of the substitution of Russian gas (American and Qatari LNG, Norwegian gas). Evolution of European storage levels during the winters of 2023/2024 and projections for 2025.

**The new energy flow map:** Redirection of Russian hydrocarbons to Asia (China, India) at significant discounts. Analysis of the effectiveness of the G7 oil price cap.

**The paradoxical acceleration of the transition: Analysis of** record investments in renewable energy and nuclear power in Europe and the United States (Inflation Reduction Act ) as a strategic response to the crisis.

**2024-2025 Review:** Towards a new normal of higher and more volatile prices? The impact on industrial competitiveness, particularly in Germany.

# Chapter 4: Inflation, Interest Rates and Fragmentation of Value Chains (2023-2025)

**The battle of the central banks:** A comparative analysis of the policies of the Fed, the ECB, and the Bank of England. The persistence of core inflation in 2023 and the dilemmas of 2024/2025 between controlling inflation and the risk of recession.

**The end of easy money:** The impact of rising interest rates on real estate, venture capital and government debt.

**Value chains and " friend - shoring ":** How war accelerated the reassessment of geopolitical risks. Analysis of companies' relocation or diversification strategies (Mexico, Vietnam, Eastern Europe).

**Sector case studies:** The impact on the automotive industry (shortage of components), semiconductors and the defense industry, the big winner of the conflict.

# Chapter 5: Economic Warfare: Sanctions, Circumvention, and the Russian Economy (2023-2025)

**Anatomy of the most extensive sanctions regime in history:** Qualitative and quantitative analysis of the measures taken by Western countries.

**"Fortress Russia" put to the test:** How Russia stabilized its economy through redirected energy revenues and strict fiscal and monetary policy. Analysis of Russian GDP in 2023 and 2024.

**New trade routes:** Investigation into circumvention mechanisms via third countries (Turkey, Kazakhstan, United Arab Emirates, China).

**Outlook 2025:** The long-term impact of sanctions on Russia's growth potential (brain drain, loss of access to technologies). Is a war economy sustainable?

# Chapter 6: The Global South: Between Alignment and Opportunism

**The losers:** Energy and food importing countries heavily impacted by the price crisis and the rising dollar. Analysis of the debt crisis in several African and Asian countries.

**The winners and the opportunists:** Hydrocarbon exporting countries (Middle East, United States). Turkey's role as a mediator and trade hub. India's position, benefiting from low-priced Russian oil.

**China, an ambivalent actor:** Rhetorical support for Russia but economic caution in the face of secondary sanctions. How Beijing is taking advantage of Russia's weakening and the West's focus on Europe.

**The challenge to the Western order:** The rise of the BRICS+ and the discourse on " de-dollarization ". Analysis of concrete initiatives and their limitations to 2025.

# Chapter 7: Conclusion: Towards a Geo-economy of Blocks?

**The end of the "peace dividend":** The structural increase in military spending and its impact on public budgets.

**A fragmented world:** Confirmation of the trend towards the formation of competing economic and technological blocs (a Western bloc, a Sino-Russian bloc, and a non-aligned "South").

**The challenges of reconstruction:** Estimating the cost of rebuilding Ukraine and the international financing mechanisms under consideration. What role for frozen Russian assets?

**Final projection 2025 and beyond:** Will the post-conflict world be defined by higher inflation, lower growth, and the primacy of national security over economic efficiency?

## Introduction: The End of an Era

On February 24, 2022, as the first columns of Russian tanks crossed the Ukrainian border, the world witnessed not only the outbreak of the most serious conventional war in Europe since 1945, but also an economic explosion whose shockwaves, far from fading, continue to reshape the contours of our global system. The deafening roar of bombs over Kyiv, Kharkiv, and Mariupol signaled the end of an era. An era, certainly already fractured, but still dominated by the principles of commercial interdependence, the optimization of value chains, and the pursuit of economic efficiency as the primary driver of international relations. In a matter of hours, these principles were subordinated to a more brutal and older logic: that of power, national security, and territory.

This book aims to analyze in depth the consequences of this conflict. But it is not simply a matter of documenting yet another crisis. The ambition of this work is to defend a central thesis: the war in Ukraine was not the primary cause of the fragmentation of the global economy, but its most powerful catalyst and its most relentless accelerator. It acted like a chemical developer, highlighting the structural weaknesses of a system that was thought to be resilient and revealing the geopolitical fault lines that had been silently developing for more than a decade.

To understand the magnitude of the 2022 earthquake, it is essential to remember the state of the world on the eve of the invasion. The global economy was barely emerging, and unevenly at that, from the artificial coma induced by the COVID-19 pandemic. It was a colossus with feet of clay. Global supply chains, the planetary "just-in-time" logistical ballet that had enabled decades of lower consumer prices, were already deeply disrupted. Semiconductor shortages were crippling the automotive industry, the cost of maritime freight had skyrocketed, and bottlenecks were emerging in every sector. Meanwhile, to avert economic collapse during lockdowns, governments and central banks had injected trillions of dollars and euros into the system. This abundant liquidity, meeting a constrained supply of goods and services, had already begun to light the fuse of an inflation that many economists at the time described, with an optimism that would soon be swept away, as "transient".

The energy context was also precarious. The ecological transition, while vital, had created a paradox: investments in fossil fuels had been discouraged more quickly than renewable energies were able to take over, creating structural tension on supply. As early as autumn 2021, well before the war, gas prices in Europe reached historic highs, signaling the extreme vulnerability of the continent, and particularly of its industrial powerhouse, Germany, to its dependence on Russian gas.

Finally, on the geopolitical front, the era of the blissful hyper-globalization of the 1990s and 2000s was over. The trade war between the United States and China, initiated under the Trump administration and continued in its spirit under the Biden administration , had already cemented the return of the primacy of politics over economics. The idea that trade softens manners and that economic interdependence guarantees peace had long since been discredited. The world was entering a phase of strategic competition where technology, data, and infrastructure had become weapons.

It was in this already feverish and fractured world that the invasion of Ukraine erupted, causing not one, but three simultaneous shockwaves: an energy shock, a food shock, and a financial shock.

The energy shock was the most immediate and the most severe. Russia was not a marginal economic player; it was an energy superpower, the world's leading exporter of gas and the second largest exporter of oil. The West's attempt to use economic leverage by sanctioning Russia led Moscow to retaliate with energy. The drastic reduction in gas deliveries via the Nord Stream 1 pipeline plunged Europe into an unprecedented crisis, raising fears of rationing and widespread deindustrialization. Gas prices on the European market (TTF) increased tenfold, spilling over into overall electricity prices and fueling runaway inflation.

The food crisis followed soon after. Ukraine and Russia, often called the "breadbaskets of the world," together accounted for nearly 30% of global wheat exports, 20% of corn exports, and almost 80% of sunflower oil exports. The Russian navy's blockade of Ukrainian Black Sea ports instantly removed millions of tons of grain from the global market, causing prices to skyrocket and threatening the food security of dozens of countries, particularly in North Africa and the Middle East, which are heavily dependent on these imports.

Finally, the financial shock was unprecedented. In response to the invasion, the United States, the European Union, and their allies unleashed an arsenal of sanctions of historic proportions. The exclusion of major Russian banks from the SWIFT interbank messaging system and, above all, the freezing of nearly half of the Central Bank of Russia's foreign exchange reserves—approximately $300 billion—constituted a weaponization of global finance. Never before had the infrastructure of the international financial system, dominated by the dollar, been used so directly against a G20 economy. This decision, while justified on moral and strategic grounds by its instigators, sent a powerful signal to all the world's capitals: assets denominated in dollars or euros are not without political risk.

The year 2022 was therefore one of shock and crisis management. But 2023 and 2024 were years of adaptation, reorganization, and the emergence of a new economic normal. It is here that analysis must focus to understand the trends that will shape the outlook for 2025 and beyond.

The major energy reorganization is undoubtedly the most dramatic transformation. Faced with the abyss, Europe managed, at an exorbitant cost, to wean itself off Russian gas. It diversified its supplies by turning massively to liquefied natural gas (LNG), primarily from the United States and Qatar, and by building regasification terminals in record time. At the same time, the crisis acted as a brutal accelerator of the energy transition, with investments in renewables and energy efficiency reaching unprecedented levels. For its part, Russia carried out an equally massive pivot eastward, redirecting its oil and gas flows toward China and India, agreeing to substantial discounts to secure these new markets. The global energy map of 2025 bears no resemblance to that of 2021. It is more regional, less efficient, and flows are now dictated as much by geopolitical alignments as by market forces.

On the monetary front, the post-conflict inflationary surge forced Western central banks, led by the US Federal Reserve (Fed) and the European Central Bank (ECB), to end more than a decade of easy money. The fastest and most synchronized round of monetary tightening since the 1980s was set in motion. While this shift helped curb the inflation spike, it left deep scars. The era of zero interest rates is over. For governments, servicing the debt accumulated during the pandemic has become a much heavier burden. For businesses and households, the cost of credit has dampened investment and consumption. The debate in 2024 and 2025 is no longer about whether inflation will be brought under control, but at what cost in terms of economic growth and financial stability.

Perhaps even more profoundly, the war has instilled in the minds of policymakers and business leaders the primacy of geopolitical risk. The mantra of efficiency at all costs has been replaced by that of resilience and security of supply. This paradigm shift has a name: fragmentation. It is no longer about producing at the lowest cost, anywhere in the world, but about producing in "friendly" or "safe" countries. Concepts like " friend - shoring " (relocating to allies) or " near - shoring " (bringing production back to nearby locations) have become the watchwords of industrial strategies. Massive public policies, such as the Inflation Reduction Act (IRA) in the United States or European sovereignty plans, now aim to subsidize and protect industries deemed strategic (semiconductors, batteries, pharmaceuticals), even if it means violating the rules of free trade.

This book aims to explore these transformations in depth, by answering a series of crucial questions for our economic future:

- How has "Fortress Russia", despite unprecedented sanctions, managed to keep its economy afloat, and is this resilience sustainable?
- Who are the winners and losers in this new situation within the "Global South"? How do countries like India, Turkey, or the Gulf monarchies navigate between blocs to come out on top?
- the " weaponization " of the dollar and the euro actually accelerate the " de-dollarization " efforts led by China and the BRICS, or do these initiatives remain marginal?
- Have we entered a new arms race, where the end of the "peace dividend" will result in a lasting displacement of civilian investment in favor of military spending?
- Finally, what will the global economy look like in 2025? Is it doomed to weaker growth, more volatile inflation, and permanently weakened international cooperation?

To answer these questions, this book is structured into seven chapters, each addressing a facet of this great transformation.

Chapter **1, "The World Economy on the Eve of Conflict"** , will paint a picture of a global system already under strain, weakened by the pandemic, the first inflationary surges and the rise of geopolitical rivalries, preparing the ground for the coming shock.

Chapter **2, "The Shockwave of 2022"** , will dissect in detail the immediate crisis through the triple prism of energy, food and finance, showing how these three crises have mutually reinforced each other.

Chapter **3, "The Great Energy Reorganization"** , will analyze the dramatic and lasting reshaping of the global energy map, Europe's pivot away from Russia, and the acceleration of the green transition as a national security imperative.

Chapter **4, "Inflation, Interest Rates and Fragmentation of Value Chains"** , will explore how the shock spread throughout the economy, forcing a change in the monetary regime and accelerating the shift from a globalization of efficiency to a globalization of security.

Chapter **5, "Economic Warfare"** , will offer a lucid analysis of the effectiveness of sanctions against Russia, the circumvention strategies put in place by Moscow, and the long-term sustainability of its war economy.

Chapter **6, "The Global South: Between Alignment and Opportunism"** , will shift away from the Western perspective to examine how emerging powers and developing countries are experiencing this new era of confrontation, between constraints and new opportunities.

Finally, the **Conclusion, "Towards a Geo-economics of Blocs?"** , will synthesize the lessons learned from the conflict to outline the contours of a new world economic order, potentially less integrated, more conflictual, and where geopolitical logic will prevail over economic rationality for a long time.

This book is an invitation to understand that we are not simply living through a period of turbulence, but rather a paradigm shift. The rules of the economic game that have governed the world for thirty years are being rewritten before our very eyes. Understanding these new rules is not merely an academic exercise; it is an imperative for citizens, businesses, and governments who must navigate this more uncertain and dangerous world. The war in Ukraine has opened a new chapter in economic history. This book aims to provide the initial keys to understanding it.

# Chapter 1: The World Economy on the Eve of Conflict: A Colossus with Feet of Clay (2020-2022)

To grasp the magnitude and nature of the economic upheavals triggered by the invasion of Ukraine on February 24, 2022, a fundamental error would be to view the event as a sudden catastrophe that struck a healthy and stable global system. Such a perspective is a hindsight illusion. The truth is that the global economy at the beginning of 2022 was anything but a healthy organism. On the contrary, it was a precarious convalescent, a colossus of impressive dimensions whose foundations, eroded by a series of pre-existing crises and tensions, were alarmingly fragile. The war did not create the crisis; it acted as a brutal detonator on an already unstable structure, targeting its most critical points of vulnerability with diabolical precision. This chapter aims to assess the health of this tottering colossus, to examine the cracks that were already running through its body before the fatal impact. Because it is by understanding these prior fragilities – the poorly healed scars of the pandemic, the precarious balance of the energy transition, and the advanced erosion of the liberal geopolitical order – that we can truly grasp why the Ukrainian shockwave was so devastating and its consequences so profound and lasting.

**The Scars of the Pandemic: Fractured Supply Chains, Abysmal Debt and Latent Inflation**

When the SARS-CoV-2 virus swept across the world in 2020, it brought the global economy to a standstill. Synchronized lockdowns brought entire sectors of production and consumption to a halt. Then, the unprecedentedly large-scale policy response acted like a defibrillator. Governments in developed countries deployed massive fiscal stimulus packages—the European "whatever it takes" approach, the American CARES Act —injecting trillions of dollars to support household incomes and keep businesses afloat. Simultaneously, central banks slashed interest rates to historic lows and flooded financial markets with liquidity through quantitative easing programs of gargantuan proportions.

This intervention prevented an economic depression comparable to that of the 1930s, but it left three deep and interconnected scars.

The first, and most visible at the end of 2021, was the dramatic disruption of global supply chains. The "just-in-time" logistics system, perfected over three decades to minimize storage costs and maximize efficiency, proved extraordinarily fragile in the face of a shock of such magnitude. The post-lockdown economic recovery was asymmetrical and chaotic. Consumer demand, frustrated by the inability to spend on services (restaurants, travel, leisure) and fueled by government aid, shifted massively toward durable consumer goods: electronics, furniture, and sporting goods. This surge in demand collided head-on with a production and transportation supply still paralyzed by health restrictions, factory closures in Asia, and labor shortages.

The result was global logistical chaos. Lines of container ships stretched for miles off the coast of major ports like Los Angeles and Shanghai. The cost of shipping a container between Asia and Europe increased tenfold, from less than $2,000 before the pandemic to nearly $20,000 at its peak. This "bullwhip effect," where a small fluctuation in final demand causes increasingly large swings upstream in the supply chain, created cascading shortages. The most emblematic was that of semiconductors. The temporary closure of a few factories in Asia, combined with a surge in demand for computers, game consoles, and servers, created a bottleneck that brought entire industries to their knees, most notably the automotive industry. Factories in Europe and North America had to shut down, not for lack of orders, but for lack of electronic chips worth a few dollars. At the beginning of 2022, the global production system was therefore deeply out of sync, creating structural inflationary pressure on the supply side.

The second scar was the burden of a colossal debt. The massive interventionism of 2020-2021 was financed by credit. According to the International Monetary Fund (IMF), global public debt surged to nearly 100% of global GDP, a level never before seen in peacetime. This rapid accumulation of debt, while necessary in the short term, created a major vulnerability. It made public finances extremely sensitive to any rise in interest rates. As long as the cost of borrowing remained close to zero, this burden was manageable. But a persistent inflationary shock was all it took to force central banks to change course and transform this debt into a fiscal trap, drastically limiting governments' ability to respond to future crises. Corporate debt had also ballooned, making the productive sector more fragile in the face of tighter credit conditions.

The third scar, a direct consequence of the first two, was the resurgence of inflation. In late 2021 and early 2022, consumer price indices surged in most advanced economies, far exceeding central banks' 2% targets. A heated debate raged among economists. For central bankers, such as Jerome Powell at the US Federal Reserve (Fed) and Christine Lagarde at the European Central Bank (ECB), this phenomenon was largely "transient." Their diagnosis rested on the idea that this inflation was primarily a supply-side phenomenon, caused by post-pandemic bottlenecks that would eventually dissipate. They underestimated the impact of demand, fueled by stimulus packages, and the risk of triggering "wage-price spirals," where employees demand wage increases to compensate for the loss of purchasing power, pushing companies to raise their prices in turn. This misdiagnosis, this belief that inflation would die out on its own, led to prolonged inaction on monetary policy. On the eve of the war, the Fed was only just beginning to signal a future tightening, while the ECB was still ruling out any rate hikes for 2022. The global economic behemoth was therefore not only unbalanced, but its guardians had their hands tied by a flawed diagnosis and the fear of derailing a still fragile recovery.

**The Energy Transition: A Precarious Balance and a Strategic Dependence**

The second major point of vulnerability in the global economy lay in the energy sector. The world was engaged, at least in theory, in a historic transition aimed at decarbonizing its economies. However, at the beginning of 2022, this transition was in a particularly perilous phase, a structurally unstable "in-between."

On the one hand, political, societal, and financial pressures (via ESG criteria – Environmental, Social, and Governance) had led to chronic underinvestment in the exploration and production of new fossil fuel resources. Large Western oil and gas companies, under fire from critics, were reducing their investments in long-term projects. This trend, while beneficial from a climate perspective, was beginning to reduce the capacity of the global oil and gas supply to meet demand.

On the other hand, the development of renewable energies and the necessary infrastructure (smart grids, storage capacity) was not yet fast enough to offset this disinvestment in fossil fuels and meet the growth in global energy demand post-pandemic. Furthermore, the production of energy sources such as wind and solar is inherently intermittent, making it dependent on favorable weather conditions and requiring dispatchable energy sources, such as natural gas or nuclear power, to ensure grid stability.

This paradox created a structural imbalance that became glaringly apparent as early as autumn 2021. A cold winter in Asia and weak wind power production in Europe were enough to trigger extreme tension in the global liquefied natural gas (LNG) market and a dramatic surge in gas prices in Europe. The price on the Dutch benchmark hub, the TTF, increased fivefold between summer and winter 2021, reaching historic highs well before the first Russian soldier crossed the border. This crisis before the crisis revealed Europe's, and particularly Germany's, critical dependence on Russian gas. Berlin, having decided to accelerate its nuclear phase-out after the Fukushima disaster, had based its entire transition strategy on Russian gas, considered a cheap and abundant transitional energy source while awaiting the full deployment of renewables. The Nord Stream 2 pipeline, completed but not yet operational, symbolized this strategic dependence.

Moscow was fully aware of this vulnerability. As early as the end of 2021, the gas giant Gazprom began to fail to meet its storage obligations in Europe and to limit its sales on the spot market, contributing to the exacerbation of rising prices. Energy had already become a weapon in the pressure tactics preceding the invasion. The global, and especially European, energy system was therefore a powder keg. It only took a spark for prices to explode and threaten to paralyze the continent's industrial activity.

**The Erosion of the Geopolitical Order: The End of Happy Globalization**

The third structural crack was geopolitical. The architecture of global governance, inherited from the post-Cold War era and based on the rule of law, multilateralism, and free trade as drivers of peace and prosperity, was in a state of advanced decay. The period that could be described as "hyper-globalization" had ended with the 2008 financial crisis, but the 2010s saw this erosion accelerate.

The central focus of this new era was the strategic rivalry between the United States and China. The illusion of China's convergence toward the liberal market economy model had dissipated, replaced by the realization in Washington of a competition for technological, economic, and military hegemony. The trade war initiated by the Trump administration starting in 2018, with its waves of punitive tariffs, marked a turning point. For the first time since the creation of the World Trade Organization (WTO), the principles of free trade were openly subordinated to national security imperatives.

This confrontation was not limited to trade. It had morphed into a fierce "tech war." The US campaign against Huawei over the deployment of 5G, restrictions on semiconductor exports to China, and the competition for dominance in artificial intelligence had fractured the global digital ecosystem. The concept of technological "decoupling," once theoretical, was becoming a reality, forcing countries and companies to choose sides. This binary logic was beginning to extend beyond technology, advocating the relocation of strategic industries and the reconfiguration of value chains to move them away from China's sphere of influence.

This intense rivalry paralyzed multilateral institutions. The WTO, deprived of its dispute settlement body by the American obstruction, was no longer able to play its role as arbiter. The G20 was divided, and consensus on major global issues, from climate change to financial regulation, became impossible. In this context, realpolitik and raw power dynamics took precedence over common rules. This climate of confrontation and widespread mistrust created an international environment where the use of economic weapons (sanctions, tariffs, export controls) became commonplace, and where military aggression, while shocking, no longer appeared as an absolute impossibility.

**The Strategic Position of Russia and Ukraine: Critical Nodes**

Finally, the Ukrainian tragedy owes its global economic significance to the unique position the two belligerents occupied in the global flow of raw materials. Neither Russia nor Ukraine were economic giants in terms of GDP (Russia's GDP was comparable to Italy's, Ukraine's to Portugal's). Their importance lay not in the size of their economies, but in their role as indispensable suppliers of essential commodities for the functioning of industry and the feeding of the world.

Russia, as we have seen, was an energy superpower, the world's leading exporter of natural gas, second in oil, and third in coal. But its critical importance didn't end there. It was also a dominant supplier of many industrial metals. It controlled approximately 40% of global palladium production (essential for catalytic converters in cars), nearly 20% of high-purity nickel (crucial for electric vehicle batteries), and was a major producer of aluminum, copper, and titanium. Furthermore, together with Belarus, it was a dominant player in the fertilizer market, particularly in potash, on which a large part of global agriculture depends. Russia was therefore not just Europe's "gas station"; it was a strategic hardware store and agricultural cooperative for the entire world.

Ukraine, for its part, was one of the world's breadbaskets. Its extraordinarily fertile black soils made it an agricultural giant. Before the war, it accounted for approximately 12% of global wheat exports, 16% of corn exports, 18% of barley exports, and, most importantly, nearly 50% of the global sunflower oil trade. Many countries, particularly in North Africa, the Middle East, and Southeast Asia, were structurally dependent on Ukrainian grain to feed their populations. The United Nations World Food Programme, which assists the most vulnerable populations, sourced more than 50% of its supplies from Ukraine. Beyond agriculture, Ukraine also possessed a significant industrial base. It was a major producer of iron ore and steel. More specifically, it was the world's leading supplier of noble gases, such as neon, a purified gas essential for the operation of lasers used in the lithography process for semiconductor manufacturing.

Thus, the theater of conflict was not a peripheral region of the global economy. It was the junction of several vital arteries. A war in Ukraine could only cause a simultaneous hemorrhage in the energy, metals, grain, and even high-technology markets.

In conclusion, the global economy that received news of the Russian invasion on February 24, 2022, was anything but resilient. It was a complex system, desynchronized by the pandemic, heavily indebted, and already plagued by nascent inflation. Its energy system was in a perilous limbo, and its geopolitical superstructure was undermined by great power competition. The conflict was not a spark on a parched plain; it was a detonator placed at the heart of an ammunition factory. It struck precisely where the system was most vulnerable: on the energy on which Europe depended, on the food supply that threatened to destabilize countries in the Global South, and on the already fractured international order. The colossus was already on shaky ground. The shock of war would bring it to its knees. The next chapter will analyze the nature and dynamics of this brutal collapse.

# Chapter 2: The Shockwave of 2022: The Triple Shock to Energy, Food, and Finance

While the first chapter painted a portrait of an economic colossus with feet of clay, this chapter focuses on the precise moment the ground gave way beneath it. On February 24, 2022, war broke out on two simultaneous fronts. The first, visible and tragic, unfolded on the plains and in the cities of Ukraine, with its tanks, missiles, and human tragedies. The second, invisible but just as devastating, erupted instantly in global markets. It was a war waged by terabytes of data, price signals, and political decisions made in the heat of the moment by capitals. The invasion of Ukraine did not trigger a classic economic crisis; it unleashed a polycrisis , a perfect storm where three distinct crisis fronts—energy, food, and finance—opened simultaneously, feeding and amplifying each other in a destructive feedback loop. The year 2022 will go down in economic history as the year of this triple shock, an earthquake whose three epicenters—Moscow, Kyiv, and Brussels—sent shockwaves to the farthest corners of the planet, from German factories to Egyptian homes, by way of Wall Street trading floors. Analyzing the mechanics of this initial explosion is essential to understanding the lasting reconfiguration of the global economy that followed.

**The Energy Shock: Europe on the Brink**

The first and most violent shock was the energy crisis. Europe discovered, with the brutality of waking up in the middle of the night, that the foundations of its industrial prosperity rested on a Faustian bargain. For decades, the economic model of its leading power, Germany, had been built on access to abundant and cheap Russian energy, a major competitive advantage for its chemical, automotive, and manufacturing industries. This interdependence, long presented as a guarantee of peace and stability—"you don't wage war on your customers and suppliers"—proved to be a gaping strategic vulnerability. Russia was not simply a supplier; it provided nearly 40% of the European Union's gas consumption.

When Western sanctions began to rain down on Moscow, the Kremlin immediately understood that its most powerful counter-weapon was not military, but energy-related. The Nord Stream 1 gas pipeline, a vital artery linking Siberia to Germany, became the instrument of strategic blackmail. Invoking technical pretexts—maintenance delays on turbines allegedly held up in Canada due to sanctions—Gazprom, the Russian state-controlled gas giant, began methodically reducing the flow. By June 2022, deliveries had been cut by 60%. In July, after a period of maintenance, they had resumed at only 20% of capacity. At the end of August, the tap was turned off for good. Each announcement of a reduction sent shockwaves through the markets.

The reaction was pure and simple panic on the European gas markets. The reference price, the Dutch TTF, which had hovered around €20 per megawatt-hour (€/ MWh ) a year earlier, skyrocketed. It crossed the €100/ MWh mark in March, reaching an unprecedented and unprecedented peak of over €340/ MWh in August 2022. This explosion in gas prices was immediately transmitted, through a kind of mechanical contagion effect, to electricity prices. In the European marginal pricing system (" meritorder "), the cost of the last power plant called upon to meet demand sets the price for all producers. And this power plant is very often a gas-fired plant. Thus, even countries not very dependent on Russian gas for their own consumption, such as France with its nuclear power plants or Spain with its LNG terminals, saw their electricity prices explode, because they were indexed to a pan-European gas price dictated by panic.

The consequences of this surge were catastrophic. For households, it translated into skyrocketing heating and electricity bills, creating a cost-of-living crisis of unprecedented scale since the oil shocks of the

1970s and threatening to plunge millions into energy poverty. For industries, it was a matter of survival. The most energy-intensive sectors were the first to be hit. Fertilizer producers, who use natural gas as a raw material, had to reduce their production by more than 70% in Europe, foreshadowing the coming food crisis. Chemical industries, such as the German giant BASF, warned that a complete shutdown of Russian gas could cause a "sudden halt" to their entire production, with cascading consequences across almost all industrial value chains (automotive, pharmaceuticals, construction). Glassworks, steel mills, paper mills: the entire European production system was threatened. The word "deindustrialization" was no longer a theoretical concept but a tangible and immediate risk.

Faced with what amounted to an "economic Armageddon," European governments reacted urgently with plans worth hundreds of billions of euros. These included "tariff shields" to protect consumers, massive subsidies for businesses, energy conservation plans, and a frantic race to find alternative supply sources. Fleets of LNG carriers transporting LNG, primarily from the United States, were diverted to Europe at exorbitant prices. Germany launched the construction of floating regasification terminals in record time. But by 2022, these solutions were merely stopgap measures. The shock had been absorbed, and Europe had realized that its post-Cold War model of prosperity was dead.

**Food Shock: Hunger as a Weapon of War**

Simultaneously with the energy crisis, a second front of crisis opened in the Black Sea. From the very first hours of the invasion, the Russian navy imposed a de facto blockade on the Ukrainian ports of Odessa, Chornomorsk, and Mykolaiv , through which the bulk of the country's agricultural exports passed. This blockade instantly removed one of its main "breadbaskets" from the global market. More than 20 million tons of grain were trapped in Ukrainian silos, held hostage by the conflict.

The impact on global agricultural commodity markets was immediate and brutal. Wheat prices on the Chicago Board of Trade (CBOT) jumped by more than 60% in a matter of weeks, reaching historic highs. Prices for corn and sunflower oil, of which Ukraine was the world's leading exporter, followed the same trajectory. The crisis was not limited to Russia's actions in Ukraine. Moscow also used its own exports as a weapon, imposing quotas and tariffs to ensure that its "friendly countries" would be served first, while leaving its deliveries to the rest of the world uncertain.

Furthermore, the energy shock directly fueled the food crisis through another channel: fertilizers. Nitrogen fertilizer production is extremely gas-intensive. The surge in gas prices in Europe therefore made production unprofitable, leading to the aforementioned factory shutdowns. At the same time, Russia and its ally, Belarus, are dominant players in the potash market, another essential component of fertilizers. Sanctions imposed on these two countries severely disrupted global supply chains. This dual fertilizer crisis caused prices to skyrocket, threatening not only the 2022 harvest but also agricultural yields in the years to come, as many farmers worldwide, particularly in developing countries, could no longer afford to fertilize their fields.

The consequences of this double shock to food and agricultural input prices have been dramatic, particularly for the most vulnerable countries. North African and Middle Eastern nations, such as Egypt (the world's largest wheat importer), Lebanon (which imported more than 80% of its wheat from the Black Sea region), and Tunisia, have faced a double blow: soaring prices for their vital food imports and an increased cost of food subsidies, against a backdrop of already depleted public finances. The threat of hunger has once again become a reality for tens of millions of people. Humanitarian agencies, such as the World Food Programme, have sounded the alarm, warning that the war in Ukraine could trigger "the most serious global food crisis since the Second World War."

The crisis also revealed the fragility of a globalized food system hyper-concentrated in the hands of a handful of major exporting countries. Food security was no longer a purely economic or humanitarian issue; it once again became, starkly, a matter of national security and sovereignty. The fear of food riots, reminiscent of the events that contributed to the outbreak of the Arab Spring in 2011, haunted diplomatic circles from Cairo to Islamabad. Diplomacy then embarked on a race against time, under the auspices of Turkey and the United Nations, to negotiate a secure grain corridor in the Black Sea, an initiative that would not materialize until the summer of 2022, after months of extreme tensions.

**The Financial Shock: The Arsenalization of the Dollar**

The third shock, more abstract but no less powerful, occurred in the intangible circuits of global finance. In response to what Western leaders described as a flagrant violation of international law, a coalition led by the United States, the European Union, the United Kingdom, and Japan unleashed an arsenal of financial sanctions of unprecedented speed and scope against an economy the size of Russia's. The objective was clear: to paralyze the Russian financial system, cause its economy to collapse, and make continuing the war unsustainable for the Kremlin.

The initial salvos were conventional, albeit far-reaching: sanctions against oligarchs and high-ranking officials, freezing of their assets, and a ban on transactions with major Russian banks such as Sberbank and VTB. The exclusion of several of these banks from the SWIFT interbank messaging system was a particularly high-profile measure. While not blocking payments per se, it made them infinitely slower, more expensive, and more complex, effectively cutting Russia off from the circulatory system of international trade.

But the most dramatic measure, the veritable financial "nuclear bomb," was the decision, made over the weekend of February 26-27, to freeze the assets of the Central Bank of Russia held in the jurisdictions of the G7 countries. Overnight, nearly $300 billion in foreign exchange reserves—roughly half of the "war chest" that Russia had meticulously accumulated for years to protect itself against shocks—became inaccessible. This decision shattered a fundamental taboo of international finance. Until then, a central bank's reserves had been considered quasi-sovereign, untouchable assets, the ultimate guarantee of a currency's and economy's stability. By freezing them, the Western powers signaled that access to the global financial infrastructure, dominated by the dollar and the euro, was not an inherent right, but a privilege conditional upon respecting the geopolitical order they upheld.

The immediate impact in Russia was seismic. The ruble lost nearly 50% of its value against the dollar in the days that followed, falling to historically low levels. The Russian population, wary after past crises, rushed to ATMs to withdraw cash, triggering scenes of bank panic. To stem the bleeding, the Central Bank of Russia, headed by Elvira Nabiullina , had to take draconian emergency measures: the Moscow Stock Exchange was closed for several weeks, the key interest rate was raised from 9.5% to 20% overnight, and extremely strict capital controls were imposed, notably requiring exporters to convert 80% of their foreign currency earnings into rubles.

On global markets, the financial shock spread through risk aversion. Investors massively abandoned assets deemed risky, seeking refuge in traditional safe havens: gold, the Swiss franc, and, paradoxically, the US dollar. The greenback appreciated dramatically, not despite the fact that the United States was orchestrating the crisis, but precisely because, in times of global crisis, it remains the ultimate safe haven. This dollar appreciation had perverse effects, notably by increasing the cost of raw material imports (priced in dollars) and the servicing of dollar-denominated debt for dozens of emerging and developing countries, thus exacerbating their energy and food shocks.

Simultaneously, the shock triggered a wave of massive divestment by Western companies. Energy giants like BP and Shell announced their withdrawal from Russian projects worth tens of billions of dollars.

Automakers like Renault sold their assets for a symbolic ruble. Hundreds of companies, from McDonald's to Ikea, suspended operations under the combined pressure of sanctions, logistical difficulties, and public opinion. In a matter of months, thirty years of Russia's integration into the global economy were undone.

**Conclusion: The Perfect Storm and the End of Innocence**

The year 2022 was thus marked by a chain reaction. The three shocks—energy, food, and financial—were not isolated events, but facets of the same systemic crisis. Rising energy prices caused fertilizer costs to skyrocket, which in turn exacerbated the food crisis. The strengthening dollar, a consequence of the financial shock, made energy and food imports even more expensive for poor countries. Sanctions disrupted the supply chains of all raw materials, from aluminum to palladium, adding inflationary pressures across all sectors.

This perfect storm abruptly ended the era of the "Great Moderation," a period of decades characterized by low inflation and stable growth, and ushered the world into a new regime of macroeconomic volatility. It revealed that the efficiency of the globalized system had been built at the expense of its resilience. Interdependence, once seen as a virtue, emerged as a vulnerability.

More profoundly, 2022 marked the end of innocence, the end of the idea that the economic sphere could be isolated from the geopolitical sphere. Capital flows, trade routes, payment systems, and access to raw materials all became instruments in a global power struggle. The shock was absorbed, leaving the global economy reeling and permanently transformed. The question then became not when the world would return to normal, but what the new normal would look like as it emerged from the ruins. It is the painful process of adaptation and reconstruction in the face of this new reality, beginning with the major energy reorganization, that the following chapter sets out to explore.

# Chapter 3: The Great Energy Reorganization (2023-2025)

The year 2022 was one of shock, disbelief, and day-to-day survival. In the autumn of that year, Europe was bracing for the worst. The most dire scenarios circulated in chancelleries and boardrooms: gas rationing, cascading production shutdowns, blackouts, a winter of social unrest. The question was not whether the European economy would enter a recession, but how deep the abyss would be. Yet, Armageddon did not occur. The crisis, though unprecedented in its severity, did not trigger the feared systemic collapse. On the contrary, it set in motion the fastest and most profound reorganization of the global energy landscape since the oil shocks of the 1970s.

The years 2023 and 2024 were not a return to normalcy—that pre-war "normal" being dead and buried—but rather a period of frenetic adaptation and structural reconstruction. This era saw Europe orchestrate a forced weaning from Russian gas at a speed no one would have thought possible, Russia pivot massively toward Asia to find new markets for its pariah hydrocarbons, and the transition to green energy paradoxically receive its most powerful boost yet. However, this major reorganization, born of pain and urgency, has given rise to a new global energy balance for 2025 and beyond: a more fragmented, more costly, more volatile, and fundamentally geopolitical balance, the consequences of which on the industrial competitiveness of major economic blocs are only now beginning to be felt.

**Europe's Great Weaning: A Race Against Time Won at a Gold Price**

At the heart of this transformation lies Europe's logistical and political feat. In less than eighteen months, the continent managed to replace nearly 155 billion cubic meters of Russian gas, an amount that, in 2021, seemed as essential to its economic metabolism as oxygen is to the human body. This achievement rests on a three-pronged approach implemented in parallel: a massive diversification of supplies, a significant reduction in demand, and a test of internal solidarity.

**The LNG Armada and the New Suppliers**

The cornerstone of this new supply strategy was Liquefied Natural Gas (LNG). A veritable armada of LNG carriers converged on European shores, radically transforming global flows. The United States, bolstered by its shale gas revolution, established itself as the new key supplier for European energy security. Its LNG exports to Europe more than doubled, making Washington the big geopolitical and commercial winner of the crisis. Qatar, another LNG giant, also strengthened its position, signing new long-term contracts with major European energy companies.

To accommodate this gas, Europe had to develop the necessary infrastructure in record time. Germany, which had no LNG import terminals at the beginning of 2022, alone symbolized this race against time. Projects that normally took nearly a decade were completed in less than a year. Floating Storage and Regasification Units (FSRUs) were installed in Wilhelmshaven, Brunsbüttel , and Lubmin , becoming the new gateways for non-Russian gas into the heart of the continent's industrial powerhouse. The Netherlands, Finland, France, and Italy followed suit, drastically increasing the continent's regasification capacity.

Meanwhile, other pipeline suppliers played a crucial role. Norway, already a reliable partner, increased its production to become Europe's leading gas supplier, a title held by Russia for half a century. The Southern Gas Corridor, carrying gas from Azerbaijan via Turkey, also saw increased flows.

However, this newfound security came at an exorbitant cost. To attract LNG shipments, European buyers had to pay top dollar on the global spot market, competing directly with Asian buyers. During the peak of the crisis in 2022, Europe paid five to ten times more for its gas than the long-term prices it had been receiving from Russia. This "freedom tax" represented a transfer of wealth worth hundreds of billions of euros from Europe to global gas producers. It also had dramatic consequences for poorer emerging countries, such as Pakistan and Bangladesh, which, unable to compete with European purchasing power, were squeezed out of the LNG market, suffering energy shortages and widespread power outages. Europe's energy deprivation was thus partly paid for by the energy insecurity of the Global South.

**The "Destruction of Demand": Between Sobriety and Deindustrialization**

The second key to European success was a drastic reduction in gas consumption, on the order of 15% to 20% compared to the average of previous years. This decrease resulted from a combination of proactive policies and drastic economic measures.

Energy conservation campaigns ("Every Little Helps") and financial incentives have played a role, encouraging households and businesses to lower their heating, optimize their consumption, and invest in energy efficiency. But a substantial part of this decrease stems from a more worrying phenomenon: the "destruction of industrial demand." Faced with unsustainable energy prices, many factories in the most energy-intensive sectors (chemicals, fertilizers, metallurgy, ceramics, paper) have had no choice but to reduce production or even temporarily cease operations.

While this destruction of demand helped balance the market and fill European gas storage facilities to record levels before the winters of 2023/2024 and 2024/2025, it left deep scars on the continent's industrial fabric. It formalized a loss of structural competitiveness, particularly for German industry, whose model relied on low energy costs. The question for 2025 and beyond is what proportion of this industry will be able to restart in an environment of persistently higher energy prices than in the United States or China.

**Russia's Pivot to the East: A New Energy Silk Road**

While Europe was frantically turning away from its hydrocarbons, Russia was carrying out an equally massive, albeit forced, strategic pivot to the East. Having lost its most solvent customer, the Kremlin had to find new outlets for its oil and gas in order to continue financing its war effort and maintaining the stability of its economy.

**Oil, Price Caps and the "Ghost Fleet"**

Oil, easier to transport by sea than gas by pipeline, was at the heart of this reorientation. The West's main weapon for limiting Moscow's revenues was the price cap mechanism , implemented by the G7 in December 2022. The idea was ingenious: to prohibit Western companies (particularly Greek shipowners and British insurers who dominate global shipping) from providing services for transporting Russian oil, unless it was sold at a price below a ceiling set at $60 per barrel. The objective was not to block Russian exports—which would have caused a surge in global prices—but to reduce the Kremlin's profit margin.

In practice, the effectiveness of this mechanism has proven mixed and has diminished over time. Initially, it worked, forcing Russia to sell its Ural crude at a substantial discount (up to $30-40) compared to Brent, the international benchmark. But Moscow quickly developed sophisticated circumvention strategies. Russia assembled a "ghost fleet" of hundreds of aging tankers, purchased through shell companies and operating outside the Western insurance system. These vessels employ concealment tactics, such as transferring cargo from ship to ship on the high seas or disabling their transponders to mask their routes.

The main beneficiaries of this new trade were China and India. These two Asian giants, refusing to comply with Western sanctions, seized the opportunity to massively purchase cheap Russian oil. By 2024, nearly 90% of Russian crude exports by sea were destined for these two countries, compared to less than 30% before the war. This pivot reconfigured maritime energy routes, but it also changed the power dynamics. Russia, which could once dictate its terms to a multitude of European buyers, now finds itself in a position of dependence on two major clients, Beijing and New Delhi, who have free rein to negotiate prices to their advantage.

**Gas: The Siberian Bottleneck**

While the shift away from oil was relatively successful, the reorientation of gas exports proved far more complex. Unlike oil, natural gas relies heavily on fixed and extraordinarily expensive infrastructure: gas pipelines. The vast gas fields of Western Siberia, which supplied Europe via the Yamal and Nord Stream pipelines, have no direct connection to the Chinese market.

The only existing infrastructure is the "Power of Siberia 1" gas pipeline, which connects the fields of Eastern Siberia to China and whose capacity is far less than the volumes that were previously sent to Europe. Moscow's major project is now the construction of a second mega-pipeline, "Power of Siberia 2," which would connect the same fields that supplied Europe to the Chinese market via Mongolia. However, negotiations with Beijing are dragging on. China, aware of its position of strength, is in no hurry. It is diversifying its own supplies (notably through LNG and Turkmen gas) and can afford to dictate its terms, particularly on price, to a Russia desperately seeking new markets. By 2025, it is clear that Russia will not be able to compensate for the loss of the European gas market. Its status as a gas superpower has been permanently diminished.

**The Paradoxical Accelerator: Security as the Engine of the Green Transition**

The 2022 energy crisis, although born of dependence on fossil fuels, paradoxically became the most powerful catalyst for the transition to decarbonized energy . The war brought about a fundamental shift in the mindset of policymakers. The argument for renewable energy shifted. It was no longer just about climate—a long-term goal, often perceived as abstract—but about national security, sovereignty, and economic survival—immediate and tangible imperatives. Breaking free from Russian gas and breaking free from fossil fuels became one and the same quest.

**REPowerEU : Europe on the Forced March**

In Europe, this new doctrine was embodied in the REPowerEU plan , launched in May 2022. This plan set extraordinarily ambitious targets to accelerate the deployment of renewable energies, double the pace of energy-efficient building renovations, and launch a large-scale green hydrogen sector. Crucially, it was accompanied by measures to drastically simplify and expedite permitting procedures for new wind and solar farms, long considered the main obstacle to their development.

The results were spectacular. 2023 and 2024 saw record numbers of solar and wind power installations across the European Union. For the first time ever, in 2023, renewable energy generated more electricity in Europe than natural gas. Solar power, in particular, experienced exponential growth, fueled by its continued decline in cost and its ease of installation for both households and businesses. This acceleration, however, has highlighted new dependencies, notably China's overwhelming dominance across the entire solar panel value chain—a strategic vulnerability that is receiving increasing attention in Brussels.

**The Inflation Reduction Act (IRA): The American Response**

On the other side of the Atlantic, the American response took the form of the Inflation Reduction Act (IRA), a misleadingly named law that is actually the largest investment plan in green technologies in US history. With nearly $370 billion in subsidies and tax credits, the IRA aims to massively stimulate the domestic production of electric vehicles, batteries, solar panels, wind turbines, and green hydrogen.

Unlike the European approach, the IRA is an openly protectionist policy that makes most of its benefits conditional on local content requirements ("made in America "). This law triggered a wave of massive investment in the United States, but it also provoked the anger of its allies, particularly European and South Korean ones, who saw it as unfair competition and a violation of international trade rules. The major energy restructuring thus opened a new front of trade tensions between Western democracies, each seeking to attract the green industries of tomorrow and secure its own supply chains.

**Conclusion: The New Energy Balance for the 2025 Horizon**

At the end of this period of abrupt transformation, the global energy landscape of 2025 is unrecognizable. A new equilibrium has emerged, not a return to stability, but a new normal characterized by structural fragility. This equilibrium rests on three pillars.

First, **energy prices are permanently higher and more volatile** , particularly for Europe. The anchor provided by cheap Russian gas has disappeared. The price of gas in Europe is now determined by the marginal cost of imported LNG, making it vulnerable to the slightest disruption in the global market: a strike at a liquefaction terminal in Australia, a cold snap in Asia, or a hurricane in the Gulf of Mexico can now trigger price spikes worldwide.

Secondly, **a fragmented and geopolitical energy market** . The idea of a unified global market optimized solely by price is dead. Energy flows now follow geopolitical fault lines. We are witnessing the emergence of blocs: a transatlantic bloc secured by American LNG, a Sino-Russian bloc based on a necessary interdependence, and a "Global South" that has become a commercial battleground where these blocs vie for access to resources and markets. Security of supply now takes precedence over economic efficiency.

Third, and perhaps the most lasting consequence, **is a divergence in industrial competitiveness between the major blocs** . Europe is emerging from the crisis with a structural handicap: energy costs that will likely remain two to three times higher than those of its main competitors. The United States, energy self-sufficient and boosted by IRA subsidies, is becoming a major magnet for industrial investment, including European investment. China, while massively accelerating its green transition, continues to benefit from privileged access to Russian hydrocarbons at bargain prices and from dominance in green technology value chains. The German industrial model, the engine of European prosperity, is therefore facing an existential challenge.

Ultimately, the major energy reorganization of 2023-2025 is a story of remarkable resilience and adaptation. Europe avoided collapse and accelerated its transition. But it is also the story of the birth of a harsher world, where competition for energy has become a central component of the rivalry between major powers. The transition to a decarbonized energy system is well underway, but its trajectory will be shaped not only by climate imperatives, but also, and above all, by the ruthless logic of geoeconomics.

# Chapter 4: Inflation, Interest Rates and Fragmentation of Value Chains (2023-2025)

While the major energy reorganization was the most visible and spectacular response to the 2022 crisis, a deeper and more silent transformation was simultaneously taking place at the very heart of the global economy's operating system. The Ukrainian shock did not merely trigger a surge in commodity prices; it acted as a chemical catalyst, altering the very nature of inflation, forcing a radical shift in monetary policy, and accelerating a fundamental reassessment of the risks underlying the geography of global production. The years 2023 to 2025 witnessed this threefold metamorphosis. They saw central banks engage in a fierce battle against inflation that had become structural, putting an end to fifteen years of "magic" and easy money. This change in the monetary regime, in turn, revealed the fragility of an economic edifice built on cheap debt. Finally, and perhaps most enduringly, the geopolitical lesson of the war has cemented a new paradigm for global trade: the era of the relentless pursuit of efficiency at all costs is over, replaced by the imperative of resilience and security. This chapter analyzes this chain reaction, from the monetary sphere to the physical organization of production, a transformation that has redefined the rules of the game for states, businesses, and investors.

**The Battle of Central Banks Against the Inflationary Hydra**

At the end of 2021, inflation was a subject of academic debate, described as "transient" by the highest monetary authorities. A year later, it had become public enemy number one, a hydra threatening to devour purchasing power, destabilize societies, and undermine the credibility of institutions. The war in Ukraine played a decisive role in this transformation, changing not only the level but also the nature of inflation.

The energy and food shock of 2022 initially acted as a powerful fuel, spreading the flames of inflation far beyond gas pump prices and supermarket price tags. These unprecedented cost increases were not absorbed by corporate profit margins; they were passed on to prices across the entire economy. This is what economists call "second-round effects": the price of gas drove up the cost of fertilizers, which in turn drove up the price of bread, which prompted workers to demand wage increases to maintain their standard of living, which forced service companies to raise their own prices. Inflation, initially concentrated on a few products, thus became widespread, pervasive, and persistent.

Faced with this dynamic and the risk of inflation expectations becoming unanchored —the point at which economic agents come to believe that inflation will remain persistently high, thus perpetuating the phenomenon—central banks had to make a complete U-turn, the most abrupt in their recent history. After an implicit "mea culpa" for their initial misdiagnosis, the US Federal Reserve (Fed), closely followed by the European Central Bank (ECB) and the Bank of England, launched, starting in mid-2022, the fastest and most synchronized round of monetary tightening since Paul Volcker 's fight against the high inflation of the 1980s .

Interest rates, which had hovered near zero for over a decade, were raised at breakneck speed, jumping in just a few quarters from 0% to over 5% in the United States and over 4% in the Eurozone. This drastic measure aimed to cool the economy: by making credit more expensive, consumption and investment were curbed, thus easing pressure on prices. While this strategy succeeded in bringing the major inflation indices down from their 2022 peaks, the battle proved far more difficult than anticipated in 2023 and 2024.

The new challenge was the persistence of "core inflation," which excludes volatile energy and food prices. Even when gas prices returned to more reasonable levels, this core inflation, particularly in the services sector where wages are the main cost, remained stubbornly high . This was a sign that the inflationary poison had spread throughout the entire economic system. This tenacity forced central banks to keep interest rates high for longer than anticipated, establishing what became known as a " higher for longer" regime.

As we approach 2025, the monetary landscape is radically different from that of the pre-war era. Central banks are navigating a difficult dilemma. On the one hand, lowering rates too soon risks allowing the inflationary hydra to regain strength. On the other, keeping them too high for too long risks plunging already anemic economies into a deep recession and triggering a financial crisis. The simplicity of the 2% inflation target is being called into question, and the world must get used to living with inflation that is structurally higher and more volatile than in the previous three decades.

**The End of Easy Money and its Cascading Consequences**

This monetary paradigm shift was not simply a matter of adjusting the dial. It marked the abrupt end of a fifteen-year era, ushered in by the 2008 financial crisis, during which money was virtually free. This influx of zero-interest liquidity had profoundly shaped the global economy, encouraging risk-taking, inflating asset prices, and allowing both governments and businesses to borrow at record levels. The sudden return to a "normal" cost of money triggered a withdrawal shock whose consequences cascaded.

**The Public Debt Trap**

For governments, the impact of rising interest rates was immediate. The mountains of public debt accumulated to address the financial crisis and then the COVID-19 pandemic suddenly became much more burdensome. Every new issue of government bonds to refinance existing debt or to finance current account deficits now comes at significantly higher interest rates. For a country like Italy, whose debt exceeds 140% of GDP, a rise of just a few percentage points in interest rates translates into billions of euros in additional debt servicing costs, crowding out other essential spending in education, healthcare, and the green transition.

This crowding-out effect drastically limits governments' fiscal space to respond to future shocks, creating structural fragility.

**"Zombie" Companies Facing the Refinancing Wall**

The business environment has also been severely tested. The era of easy money had allowed many "zombie" companies to survive—unprofitable businesses that were only able to service their debts thanks to extremely low interest rates. The sharp rise in the cost of credit acted like a receding tide, revealing those that were swimming without a swimsuit. Faced with a refinancing wall, many of these companies went bankrupt in 2023 and 2024, leading to a surge in defaults and corporate restructurings.

**Vulnerable Sectors: Real Estate and Technology**

Two sectors have proven particularly vulnerable to this new regime. The first is real estate, a sector intrinsically linked to the cost of credit. Rising mortgage rates have made homeownership more difficult for households, causing a sharp slowdown in transactions and a price correction in many Western countries. Real estate developers, often heavily indebted, have found themselves in dire straits, raising fears of a broader crisis.

The second sector is technology and venture capital. The tech ecosystem , particularly its most speculative segments, had thrived in the zero-interest-rate environment. Valuations of unprofitable startups were based on the promise of very distant profits. However, a basic principle of finance is that the higher the interest rates , the less value future profits have today. Monetary tightening therefore triggered a collapse in valuations, a drying up of venture capital funding, and a wave of layoffs in the sector. The spectacular bankruptcy of Silicon Valley Bank (SVB) in March 2023, a bank specializing in financing this ecosystem, was the most striking symptom of this abrupt correction.

**From Efficiency to Resilience: The Strategic Fragmentation of Value Chains**

Beyond the monetary and financial spheres, the most structural consequence of the war in Ukraine can be seen on the map of global production. The conflict has delivered a powerful and painful lesson to business leaders and policymakers: excessive dependence on a single supplier, even the most efficient and cheapest, poses an existential risk. The blockade of Ukrainian ports, the halt in Russian gas deliveries, and the German automotive industry's reliance on wiring harnesses produced in western Ukraine were textbook examples. The "just-in-time" approach , which aimed to optimize costs by minimizing inventory and sourcing from the cheapest point in the world, has given way to the " just -in-case" approach .

This paradigm shift has given rise to a new geoeconomic lexicon:

- " **Reshoring** " **(relocation)** : The repatriation of production to the national territory.
- " **Near - shoring** " : The relocation of production to geographically close countries to shorten supply chains and limit transport risks (for example, from Mexico for the American market, from Poland or Morocco for the European market).
- " **Friend - shoring** " : The most important of these concepts, promoted by US Treasury Secretary Janet Yellen . It involves reconfiguring supply chains so that they primarily pass through countries that share the same values and geopolitical interests, thus reducing dependence on "systemic rivals" like China or Russia.

This trend is not solely driven by businesses. It is actively encouraged, even orchestrated, by states. Economic security has become an essential component of national security. Laws such as the **CHIPS and Science Act** and the **Inflation Reduction Act (IRA)** in the United States are not simply subsidy programs; they are instruments of a strategic industrial policy aimed at rebuilding a national production base in sectors deemed vital (semiconductors, batteries, renewable energy). Europe has followed suit with its own **European CHIPS Act** and its **Critical Infrastructure for Nuclear Energy (CINE) Act. RawMaterialsAct** , seeking to reduce its critical dependencies, particularly on China.

**Case Studies of Fragmentation**

This reconfiguration is already visible in several key sectors by 2024-2025:

- **The automotive industry** was one of the first to react. Having suffered from shortages of semiconductors and then Ukrainian components, it is investing heavily to create regional value chains for electric vehicle batteries. " Gigafactories " are being built at a breakneck pace in North America and Europe to reduce the overwhelming dependence on Asia.
- **Semiconductors** are at the epicenter of the geoeconomic battle. The realization that over 90% of the most advanced chips are produced in Taiwan, an island under constant threat of Chinese invasion, sent shockwaves through Washington and Brussels. Billions in public subsidies are aimed at relocating some of this strategic production, even if it takes a decade and costs significantly more.
- **The defense industry** is, by necessity, the biggest beneficiary of this new paradigm. The war emptied Western arsenals and highlighted the deindustrialization of this sector. Defense budgets have skyrocketed, and governments are placing massive orders to replenish ammunition stocks and develop next-generation equipment. This is creating a boom for the sector and effectively relocating high-tech production.

**Conclusion: The Cost of Security**

The economic world of 2025 is therefore the product of this chain reaction. The inflationary shock triggered by the war ended the era of easy money, creating a more restrictive and riskier financial environment. This environment, combined with the brutal awakening to geopolitical risks, accelerated the shift from a globalization optimized for efficiency to a fragmented globalization organized for resilience.

This new globalization, sometimes called " slowbalization " or bloc globalization, has an inherent cost. Diversification, redundancy, and production in more expensive but safer countries are, by definition, less efficient from a purely economic standpoint. This "cost of insurance" against geopolitical risk is structurally inflationary. In seeking to secure their supplies, Western economies introduce a risk premium into the price of almost all goods.

Thus, the cycle is complete. The shock of war triggered inflation that forced central banks to act. Their actions, combined with the geopolitical lessons of the conflict, led to a fragmentation of value chains. And this fragmentation, in turn, creates a foundation of structural inflation for years to come. The world has entered a new geoeconomic age, where the pursuit of security takes precedence over the pursuit of low-cost prosperity—a trade-off whose long-term consequences are only beginning to emerge.

# Chapter 5: Economic Warfare: Sanctions, Circumvention, and the Russian Economy (2023-2025)

When the first rounds of Western sanctions hit Russia in February and March 2022, a near-unanimous consensus emerged in Western capitals. The prevailing narrative was one of an "economic blitzkrieg": the financial, technological, and commercial arsenal deployed against Moscow was intended to trigger a rapid collapse of the ruble, a banking panic, a deep recession, and ultimately, make the continuation of the war effort materially impossible. French Economy Minister Bruno Le Maire declared his intention to provoke "the collapse of the Russian economy." Yet, by 2025, it is clear that this collapse has not occurred. The Russian economy, although profoundly transformed and battered, is not on its knees. It has adapted, demonstrated unexpected resilience, and even posted growth rates exceeding those of many European economies in 2023 and 2024.

This chapter aims to dissect this enigma. How did "Fortress Russia," subjected to the most severe and comprehensive sanctions regime in modern history, not only survive but also manage to reconfigure itself into a functional war economy? The analysis of this resilience focuses on three key areas: the nature of the anti-sanctions shield erected by Russian technocrats, the art of circumvention and the construction of new gray trade routes, and finally, the structural transformation of the economy toward a military-Keynesian model. However, this survival comes at an exorbitant cost and has devastating long-term consequences. This chapter will also examine the other side of the coin: technological regression, increased dependence on China, and the cannibalization of the country's economic future, which paint a picture of a Pyrrhic victory for 2025 and beyond.

**Anatomy of an Unprecedented Economic Seat**

To measure the performance of the Russian economy, one must first fully grasp the extent of the attack it has suffered. The sanctions regime implemented by the G7 and its allies is multidimensional and aimed to simultaneously attack all vital aspects of the economy.

- **The financial front** was the most brutal and immediate. Freezing the Central Bank's reserves deprived Russia of half its financial shield. Excluding major banks from the SWIFT system and prohibiting all transactions with them aimed to isolate the country from the global financial system.
- **The trade and technology front** was designed to strike for the long term. Drastic export controls were imposed to deprive Russia of access to Western technologies, especially semiconductors, aviation components, software, and advanced equipment essential for modernizing its military and industry.
- **The energy sector** , the heart of Russia's revenue-generating machine, has been attacked in successive waves. The European Union imposed an embargo on its coal imports, then on its crude oil imports by sea. The G7 subsequently implemented the oil price cap mechanism to try to reduce the Kremlin's profits without creating a global supply shock.
- **The human and industrial front** was marked by a massive and voluntary exodus of more than a thousand Western companies. This exodus, ranging from the automotive industry (Renault) to consumer goods (McDonald's) and including technology (Apple, Microsoft), represented not only a loss of investment and jobs, but also a loss of know-how, technologies and management standards.

Faced with this total siege, the Russian response was equally total, combining skillful emergency measures, strategic opportunism and a brutal reorientation of national priorities.

**"Fortress Russia" Put to the Test: Keys to Resilience**

The survival of the Russian economy in 2022 and its stabilization in 2023-2024 rest on four fundamental pillars.

**1. The Technocrats' Masterstroke:** The first line of defense was not political but technical, orchestrated by the Central Bank of Russia under the leadership of Elvira Nabiullina . Faced with the collapse of the ruble and the bank panic of March 2022, the response was remarkably effective. Doubling the key interest rate to 20%, imposing draconian capital controls (prohibiting foreigners from selling their Russian assets and limiting foreign currency outflows), and requiring exporters to convert 80% of their dollar or euro revenues into rubles created a massive artificial demand for the national currency. These measures not only halted the ruble's fall but also triggered its spectacular appreciation during 2022, which helped contain imported inflation and restore a semblance of confidence. This crisis management demonstrated the quality of a team of technocrats who, since the annexation of Crimea in 2014, had prepared for a "besieged fortress" scenario.

**2. The Paradoxical Energy Windfall:** The sanctions weapon initially backfired. The war and the uncertainty it provoked caused global oil and gas prices to skyrocket. Thus, even though Russia was forced to sell slightly lower volumes, it did so at such higher prices that its hydrocarbon export revenues reached record levels in 2022. This unexpected windfall financed a growing budget deficit, subsidized the economy, and maintained social stability. By the time European energy sanctions were fully implemented, the pivot to Asia was already well underway, allowing for the disposal of crude oil barrels that had become undesirable in Europe.

**3. "Wartime Keynesianism":** The surprise of Russia's 2023 GDP growth figures (+3.6%) and the solid forecasts for 2024 do not stem from a thriving civilian economy, but from a massive injection of public spending into the defense sector. The Russian government opened the budgetary floodgates to finance the production of munitions, tanks, missiles, and military equipment. Defense spending reached post-Soviet levels, accounting for nearly a third of the federal budget and more than 6% of GDP. Factories in the military-industrial complex operate around the clock, in three shifts, hiring massively and offering wages well above average. This colossal fiscal stimulus boosted industrial production, reduced unemployment to historically low levels, and, through a trickle-down effect, supported household consumption. Russia has transitioned from a modernizing market economy to a centralized war economy.

**4. The Substitution Effect:** The departure of Western companies created a void that was filled by two forces. On the one hand, local players bought up the abandoned assets at bargain prices, often with the Kremlin's blessing. On the other hand, and far more significantly, Chinese companies rushed into the breach. Chinese car brands ( Chery , Geely , Haval ) now dominate the Russian market, replacing Renault and Volkswagen. Smartphones from Xiaomi and Honor have taken the place of Apple and Samsung. This substitution has made it possible to maintain a supply of consumer goods and avoid the massive shortages that could have fueled social discontent.

**The New Grey Silk Roads: The Art of Circumvention**

Russia's resilience would not have been possible without the establishment of a vast and complex network for circumventing sanctions, particularly for the import of embargoed technological goods. A new trade geography emerged, based on intermediary countries that saw an economic opportunity in their non-alignment with Western policy.

Turkey, the United Arab Emirates, and the countries of Central Asia (Kazakhstan, Kyrgyzstan, Uzbekistan) and the Caucasus (Armenia, Georgia) have become the main hubs for this parallel trade. The mechanism is simple: a Russian company orders electronic chips, machine tools, or spare parts from Western countries through a shell company based in Istanbul, Dubai, or Almaty. This company legally imports the goods from Europe or the United States and then re-exports them to Russia. Customs statistics from these countries show a surge in imports of goods from the West and a corresponding surge in their exports to Russia, often for the same product categories.

This network has allowed the Russian military industry to continue procuring Western electronic components, which are found in missiles and drones recovered from the Ukrainian battlefield. It has also allowed the civilian industry to survive. China plays a pivotal role in this scheme, not only as a hub but also as a direct supplier of technological alternatives, even if these are often of inferior quality. This gray economy, although less efficient and more expensive than direct trade, has been the lifeline that has kept the Russian patient alive.

**The Hidden Cost of Survival: Perspectives to 2025**

The facade of resilience and growth in the Russian economy, however, masks deep-seated problems that seriously jeopardize its future. Short-term survival has been bought at the price of long-term structural decline. By 2025, four major costs are clearly emerging.

**1. Cannibalizing the Future:** The current war economy operates by cannibalizing the civilian economy. Investments, subsidies, and, above all, human capital (engineers, skilled technicians) are siphoned off by the military-industrial complex to the detriment of all other sectors with a promising future: healthcare, education, civilian infrastructure, telecommunications, and non-military research and development. This overheating of the defense sector creates a critical labor shortage in the rest of the economy, fuels inflation, and guarantees stagnation, or even a decline, in the standard of living for the majority of the population once the military stimulus wanes.

**2. Technological Regression:** Despite workarounds, Russia remains cut off from the Western innovation ecosystem. It can import chips, but not the ASML extreme ultraviolet lithography machines needed to manufacture them. It can fly its airliners, but by cannibalizing part of the fleet for spare parts, compromising long-term safety. In every field, from deep-sea oil extraction to cutting-edge medicine, Russia is doomed to technological decline. Its future growth potential, which depends on productivity and innovation, is therefore structurally crippled.

**3. The Aggravated Demographic Crisis:** War is a demographic disaster for a country already in decline. The hundreds of thousands of dead and wounded represent countless young men removed from the workforce and from social life. Added to this is the wave of emigration in 2022, which saw several hundred thousand of Russia's most educated and skilled citizens—computer scientists, researchers, entrepreneurs—leave, rejecting both war and repression. This double hemorrhage, both military and civilian, accelerates the aging of the population and creates an unsustainable burden on the future social and economic system.

**4. Vassalization by China:** The pivot to the East, presented by the Kremlin as a liberation from Western dependence, is in reality the exchange of interdependence for asymmetrical dependence. Russia has become a junior partner of China. It sells its hydrocarbons to China at a steep discount, making it dependent on a virtually single customer. It is adopting Chinese technological and financial standards (the CIPS payment system, Huawei technology ). The yuan is gradually replacing the dollar and the euro in Russian reserves and transactions. In the long term, Russia risks becoming a mere supplier of raw materials for China's manufacturing powerhouse, a considerable loss of economic and strategic sovereignty.

**Conclusion: A Fortress with Undermined Foundations**

In conclusion, the analysis of the Russian economy between 2022 and 2025 reveals a striking paradox. The Western "economic blitzkrieg" failed in its objective of provoking an immediate collapse. Thanks to a combination of competent crisis management, providential energy revenues, a brutal conversion to a war economy, and aid from third countries, Fortress Russia held firm . However, this fortress is being undermined from within. The economic model emerging by 2025 is more isolated, more state-controlled, more militarized, and technologically inferior to that of 2021. It is entirely focused on a single objective—supporting the war effort—at the expense of all the factors that determine a nation's long-term prosperity. Russia's resilience is not a sign of enduring strength, but rather a manifestation of its capacity to endure pain and sacrifice its own future. Economic warfare has not destroyed Russia, but it condemns it to a slow decline, impoverishing stagnation, and a second-tier position in the shadow of its powerful Chinese neighbor.

# Chapter 6: The Global South: Between Alignment and Opportunism

The war in Ukraine is often presented, through the lens of Western media and governments, as a binary confrontation: Russia against Ukraine and its NATO allies. This view, while strategically relevant, is economically and politically incomplete. It obscures the reactions, calculations, and fates of the vast majority of humanity living outside this direct axis of conflict: the diverse and complex group of nations in Asia, Africa, the Middle East, and Latin America known as the "Global South." For these countries, the war in Ukraine was not a matter of abstract moral choice or ideological alignment, but a brutal economic reality and a new landscape of strategic opportunities.

The conflict acted as a powerful revealer and accelerator of trends, exposing the vulnerabilities of some, rewarding the pragmatism of others, and offering regional powers the opportunity to assert their autonomy on the world stage. Far from provoking a monolithic alignment behind one side or the other, the war highlighted a widespread refusal on the part of the Global South to subscribe to a new Cold War logic. On the contrary, it catalyzed the quest for a multipolar world, where national interest takes precedence over the dictates of the great powers. This chapter analyzes this complex dynamic by distinguishing three categories of actors: the collateral victims of the crisis, caught in the turmoil of the triple shock; the navigators and opportunists who managed to come out on top; and finally, China, this ambivalent giant whose cautious approach was one of the determining factors in the global geoeconomic balance from 2023 to 2025.

**The Victims of the Polycrisis : The Heavy Toll on Vulnerable Nations**

For dozens of developing countries, the shockwave of 2022 was not a matter of geopolitics, but of survival. They were the innocent and helpless victims of the triple energy, food, and financial shock described in Chapter 2.

**The Double Burden of Food and Energy**

For net food and energy-importing countries, the situation quickly became untenable. Egypt, the world's largest wheat importer, which sourced over 80% of its wheat from Russia and Ukraine, was hit particularly hard. The surge in wheat prices on global markets put extreme pressure on the state budget, which heavily subsidizes bread, a staple food essential for social peace. The threat of a repeat of the "food riots" that preceded the 2011 Arab Spring became a major concern for Cairo and many other capitals in the region, such as Tunis and Beirut.

The crisis was exacerbated by soaring oil and fertilizer prices. Countries like Pakistan, Bangladesh, and Sri Lanka, already heavily indebted, saw their energy import bills skyrocket, depleting their foreign exchange reserves. The inability to procure LNG on a global market where European buyers were offering exorbitant prices led to massive power outages, paralyzing industry and daily life. This imported energy crisis had direct consequences for local agricultural production, as farmers could no longer afford fertilizers or irrigation pumps, creating a vicious cycle of dependence and vulnerability.

**The Strong Dollar and Debt Trap**

The financial shock delivered the final blow. The war triggered a global flight toward quality, that is, toward the US dollar. The dramatic strengthening of the greenback had a devastating effect on developing countries. First, because commodities are priced in dollars, every barrel of oil and every ton of wheat became even more expensive in their local currency. Second, for countries that had contracted a significant portion of their debt in dollars, each repayment became more costly, bringing them closer to default.

Sri Lanka was the first domino to fall, declaring bankruptcy in May 2022, its crisis precipitated by a soaring import bill. Other countries, such as Ghana, Zambia, and Pakistan, found themselves on the brink, forced to negotiate emergency bailouts with an International Monetary Fund (IMF) itself grappling with a wave of multiple crises. The war in Ukraine thus revealed and exacerbated a sovereign debt crisis that had been brewing since the pandemic, threatening to derail the development goals of an entire generation. For these nations, the distant conflict in Europe acted as a catalyst for poverty and instability.

**Opportunists and Balancing Powers: The Geoeconomics of Non-Alignment**

At the opposite end of the spectrum, the crisis created extraordinary opportunities for a group of "middle powers" who navigated this new polarized environment with pragmatism and agility. Their strategy was not one of passive neutrality, but of active non-alignment, playing on multiple fronts to maximize their national interests.

**The Gulf Monarchies: Oil Kings and Diplomatic Pivots**

The immediate big winners of the crisis were undoubtedly the hydrocarbon-exporting countries of the Gulf Cooperation Council (GCC). Saudi Arabia, the United Arab Emirates, and Qatar saw their energy revenues reach stratospheric heights in 2022 and 2023. This financial windfall gave them unprecedented geopolitical leverage.

Aware of their new position of strength as swing producers , they have asserted a marked strategic autonomy vis-à-vis their traditional security partner, the United States. The decision by OPEC+, the expanded cartel co-led by Riyadh and Moscow, to reduce oil production in the fall of 2022 against the explicit advice of Washington was a strong signal of this newfound confidence. Simultaneously, the Emirates, and Dubai in particular, have positioned themselves as a haven for Russian capital fleeing sanctions, while remaining an indispensable financial partner for the West. Diplomatically, they have acted as mediators in prisoner exchanges and have used their sovereign wealth funds, flush with petrodollars, to project their influence by investing heavily in strategic assets in Europe, Asia, and Africa.

**Turkey: The Ambivalent Hub**

Erdoğan 's Turkey has played a remarkably complex and ambivalent role. As a NATO member, it supported Ukraine by supplying Bayraktar drones , which proved crucial at the start of the conflict. But as a Black Sea power, it refused to implement Western sanctions and maintained a constant dialogue with the Kremlin.

This unique position has allowed Turkey to transform itself into an indispensable commercial, financial, and diplomatic hub. Ankara was the key mediator in the 2022 Ukrainian grain agreement, a major diplomatic victory. Economically, Turkey has become Russia's primary backdoor for circumventing sanctions. Turkish exports to Russia have skyrocketed, including numerous Western goods re-exported through shell companies. The country has become a hub for Russia's "ghost fleet" of oil tankers and a haven for Russian tourists and oligarchs. This dual role has allowed Turkey to serve its economic interests while simultaneously making itself indispensable on the diplomatic stage.

**India: The Champion of "Strategic Autonomy"**

Narendra Modi's India has established itself as the most successful example of the doctrine of "strategic autonomy". Historically non-aligned and keen to preserve its long-standing relations with Moscow (a major arms supplier), New Delhi firmly resisted Western pressure to condemn the invasion and implement sanctions.

India's pragmatism was primarily economic. The country saw a golden opportunity in Russian oil, which had become a pariah state. From a marginal supplier before 2022, Russia became India's leading crude oil supplier in 2023, selling its oil at a significant discount. Indian refineries operated at full capacity, importing this cheap oil, processing it into diesel, gasoline, and kerosene, and re-exporting some of these petroleum products—including to Europe, which had imposed an embargo on Russian goods. This maneuver, while legal, illustrated how trade flows reconfigure themselves to circumvent sanctions regimes. For India, the top priority was protecting its population from energy inflation and seizing a competitive advantage for its industry, regardless of the displeasure of its Western partners in the Quad (United States, Japan, Australia).

**The Giant Ambivalent: China's Calculated Game**

No actor in the Global South has held such a closely watched and decisive position as China. Bound to Russia by a "limitless" partnership proclaimed just weeks before the invasion, Beijing found itself in a delicate but strategically advantageous position. Its approach was a masterpiece of careful calculation, aimed at maximizing the benefits of the situation while minimizing the risks.

**Rhetorical Support, Material Prudence**

On the rhetorical and diplomatic front, China has consistently supported Moscow. It has abstained from votes of condemnation at the UN, adopted the Kremlin's rhetoric accusing NATO expansion of being the root cause of the conflict, and denounced unilateral Western sanctions.

However, on a practical level, caution was paramount. Beijing meticulously avoided crossing "red lines" that could have triggered secondary Western sanctions against its own institutions. Major Chinese state-owned banks largely complied with financial sanctions, and tech giants like Huawei maintained a low profile so as not to jeopardize their access to global markets, which are far more vital to them than the Russian market. China did not supply lethal weapons to Russia, limiting itself to providing dual-use goods (civilian drones, electronic components, trucks) which, while useful to the Russian war effort, remained in a gray area.

**The Strategic Dividends of the Crisis**

While exercising this caution, China has reaped significant strategic dividends from the war:

1. **A supplier of bargain-priced energy:** Like India, but on a much larger scale, China took advantage of Russia's isolation to secure massive supplies of oil, gas, and coal at very advantageous

prices. This helped control inflation within its borders and gave its manufacturing industry a competitive edge.

2. **A dependent junior partner:** The war transformed the Sino-Russian relationship. A weakened and isolated Russia became a junior partner, dependent on China for economic opportunities, access to technology, and diplomatic support. This allowed Beijing to increase its influence in Central Asia, Moscow's traditional sphere of influence, and to position itself in a stronger negotiating position on future energy projects such as the Power of Siberia 2 gas pipeline.
3. **A welcome distraction:** The total focus of the United States and Europe on the war in Ukraine has diverted their attention, resources, and strategic bandwidth from what Washington nevertheless considers its main long-term challenge: competition with China in the Indo-Pacific . This "window of opportunity" has allowed China to continue advancing its interests in the South China Sea and strengthening its ties with many countries in the region.

### Conclusion: The Advent of an "À la Carte" Order

The experience of the years 2022 to 2025 profoundly altered the perception and stance of the Global South. The war in Ukraine acted as a catalyst for collective self-assertion. The refusal to align oneself was not a sign of weakness or indifference, but rather the manifestation of a rapidly changing world order, shifting from a unipolar or bipolar model to a multipolar, or even " a-polar ," system, where nations choose their partnerships "à la carte" according to their immediate interests.

This trend has materialized in the strengthening of alternative forums to Western governance, such as the BRICS. The group's dramatic expansion in 2024 to include energy powerhouses (Saudi Arabia, UAE, Iran) and demographic heavyweights (Egypt, Ethiopia) symbolized this desire to create a counterweight to the G7's hegemony. The discourse on " de-dollarization ," although its concrete effects remain limited until 2025, has become a powerful political narrative, fueled by the fear of seeing the dollar and the Western financial system used as weapons.

Ultimately, the most profound lesson for the Global South has been that of sovereignty. The crisis has shown that in a world of great power competition, food security, energy security, and financial stability cannot be taken for granted. They must be actively sought and defended. Far from rallying the world to a common cause, the war in Ukraine has accelerated its fragmentation into fluid and pragmatic blocs of interests, outlining the contours of a new, more complex and unpredictable world order, in which the Global South is no longer a spectator but a full-fledged actor.

# Chapter 7: Conclusion: Towards a Geo-economy of Blocks?

At the end of this analytical journey, one conclusion is undeniably clear: the war in Ukraine was not simply a crisis, however violent. It was a tectonic event, a historical turning point that shattered the last illusions of the post-Cold War era. The veil of a peaceful globalization, governed by economic rationality and harmonious interdependence, was torn away for good. As we have argued throughout this book, the conflict did not so much create a new world as it brutally accelerated and rendered irreversible trends that had been brewing for over a decade: the end of hyper-globalization, the return of great power competition, and the primacy of politics over economics.

The years 2022 to 2025 were not a chaotic interlude after which a return to normalcy would be possible. They were the foundational years of a new paradigm, a new global geoeconomic order—or disorder—whose rules are currently being rewritten. This final chapter aims to synthesize the characteristics of this new world. It will acknowledge the demise of the "peace dividend," map the new global architecture fragmented into competing power blocs, examine the monumental challenge of rebuilding Ukraine, and finally, venture a projection of what our economic reality will be like by 2026 and beyond. Because navigating the world of tomorrow requires understanding that the old maps are now obsolete.

### The End of the "Peace Dividend" and the Primacy of Politics

The most fundamental transformation, the one that underpins all the others, is the end of the "peace dividend." This expression referred to the economic benefits that Western countries reaped after the fall of the Soviet Union, when they were able to drastically reduce their defense budgets and reallocate those resources to consumption, private investment, or social spending. That era is over. The war in Ukraine has served as a stark reminder that security is not a given, but a prerequisite for prosperity, and that it comes at a price.

Rearmament has become the new priority. Germany, for whom economic pacifism was a state doctrine, has undergone its *Zeitenwende* ("era change") by releasing a special fund of 100 billion euros to modernize its Bundeswehr. Poland has embarked on a military spending program that puts it at the top of NATO as a percentage of GDP. The target of 2% of GDP for defense, long considered a theoretical ceiling by many members of the Atlantic Alliance, is now seen as an essential minimum.

This reorientation has profound and lasting macroeconomic consequences. First, it crowds out public budgets. Every euro spent on a tank or a missile is a euro not invested in the ecological transition, education, civilian research, or the healthcare system. In a context of already record public debt, this rearmament can only be financed by raising taxes, reducing other spending, or increasing borrowing, creating a permanent dilemma for governments.

Secondly, this arms race creates structural inflationary pressure. The defense sector has entered a phase of overheating, with order books full for the coming decade. It is draining scarce resources, whether raw materials (steel, titanium, rare earth elements), electronic components, or, above all, human capital. The engineers, technicians, and skilled workers, massively recruited by defense giants like Rheinmetall , Thales, and BAE Systems, are no longer available for civilian industries, creating labor shortages and driving up wages.

Politics, and more specifically national security, has thus regained its primacy. Investment decisions, trade policies, and industrial strategies are now systematically evaluated through a security lens. Economic efficiency, the supreme criterion of globalization over the last thirty years, is now subordinate to the imperative of resilience and strategic autonomy. This fundamental trade-off—accepting to pay more for greater security—is the new grammar of the global economy.

**Towards a Geo-Economy of Blocks: Fragmented Globalization**

This primacy of politics has completed the fracturing of the global economic space, reorganizing it into three large competing groups whose outlines were clearly drawn between 2023 and 2025. The era of a single and fluid global market, governed by the rules of the WTO, has given way to a geo-economy of blocs.

**1. The Euro-Atlantic Bloc Unified by "De- Risking ":** Led by the United States, this bloc has significantly tightened its grip on the NATO military alliance and the G7 political forum. Its economic doctrine is one of "de- risking " (risk reduction) vis-à-vis China and the isolation of Russia. Its instruments are the " weaponization " of finance (sanctions), export controls on sensitive technologies (via laws like the CHIPS Act ), and an interventionist industrial policy aimed at relocating or " friend - shoring " strategic production chains (via the Inflation Reduction Act ). The bloc's strength lies in its technological and financial dominance (the dollar remains central). Its weakness lies in its internal contradictions, particularly the trade tensions caused by American protectionism, which penalizes its European and Asian allies (Japan, South Korea).

**2. The Sino-Russian Axis of Dispute:** The war cemented an alliance of necessity between China and a weakened Russia. This is not a unified ideological bloc like the Soviet bloc, but a transactional partnership whose main unifying force is their shared opposition to American hegemony. In this profoundly asymmetrical relationship, Russia has become a supplier of low-cost energy raw materials and a junior military partner, while China provides a vital economic outlet, alternative technologies ( Huawei , etc.), and a diplomatic umbrella. The objective of this axis is to build an alternative infrastructure to the Western order, by promoting institutions like BRICS+ and the Shanghai Cooperation Organisation, and by developing alternatives to the dollar and the SWIFT system, even if their scope remains limited.

**3. The Multi-Aligned "Global South":** The major lesson of this period is the emergence of a third pole, not as a unified bloc, but as a collective force of pragmatic non-alignment. Regional powers such as India, Brazil, Saudi Arabia, Turkey, and South Africa have refused to be drawn into a binary logic. They pursue a "pick-and-choose" foreign policy, collaborating with the West on certain issues while strengthening their economic ties with the Sino-Russian axis on others. These "pivotal states" have understood that their influence is maximized by playing each other off. They are the arena for the new geoeconomic competition, and their capacity to organize themselves, particularly through the expansion of the BRICS, makes them an essential player demanding a reform of global governance (UN Security Council, IMF, World Bank) which they consider obsolete.

This fragmentation is not without cost. The duplication of value chains, the multiplication of trade and technological barriers, and the loss of efficiency gains linked to international specialization constitute a structural brake on global growth and a source of persistent inflation.

**The Titanic Challenge of Reconstruction and the Question of Russian Assets**

At the heart of future European stability lies the fate of Ukraine. The cost of reconstruction, even before the end of hostilities, is already estimated by the World Bank and other institutions at over $500 billion, a figure that could approach $1 trillion. This 21st-century "Marshall Plan" represents a colossal financial, political, and human challenge. The central question, which dominated debates in 2024 and 2025, is that of its financing.

Three sources of funding are being considered, but all are problematic. Western public funds are constrained by high national debts and public opinion weary of supporting the war. Private investment, while essential, will only materialize on a large scale if absolute guarantees against a resumption of the conflict are offered, which seems unlikely in the short term.

There remains the third option, politically appealing but legally explosive: confiscating the approximately $300 billion in frozen assets held by the Central Bank of Russia to finance reconstruction. The "aggressor pays" principle enjoys widespread moral support. However, its implementation faces fundamental legal obstacles, notably the principle of sovereign immunity. The United States has been the most supportive of outright seizure. Europeans, particularly Belgium, where a large portion of these assets is held through the Euroclear clearing house , are far more hesitant. They fear that such a measure would set a dangerous precedent, encourage other countries (especially China and the Gulf states) to withdraw their euro-denominated reserves, and expose their own assets abroad to retaliatory measures.

The compromise solution that emerged in 2024-2025—using profits generated by frozen assets rather than the assets themselves—is a first step, but it represents only a fraction of what is needed. How this issue is resolved will be a major test for the unity of the Western bloc and for the credibility of international law. The successful reconstruction of Ukraine is not merely an economic imperative; it is a strategic imperative. A rebuilt, prosperous, democratic Ukraine integrated into the European Union would be the ultimate strategic defeat for the Kremlin. Failure would leave a gray zone of instability on Europe's doorstep for decades.

**Final Projection: The Economic World to 2026 and Beyond**

By synthesizing all these transformations, what portrait of the global economy can we sketch for 2026? The world is not on the brink of apocalypse, but it has entered a regime structurally different from the one we have known. The "new normal" will be defined by:

- **Structurally higher inflation:** The convergence of costs from fragmentation (less efficient value chains), rearmament (pressure on resources), and the energy transition (massive investments) will create an inflation floor higher than the 2% target set by central banks. Their task will become infinitely more complex.
- **Lower potential growth:** The end of hyper-globalization,

barriers to trade and investment, and the allocation of capital for security rather than productivity will weigh on long-term growth. Secular stagnation, already a concern before the war, could become a reality for many advanced economies.

- **Increased volatility and persistent geopolitical risk:** Shocks will no longer be the exception but the norm. Energy and food markets will remain points of friction. Trade tensions, cyberattacks, and regional conflicts will have immediate global economic repercussions. Managing geopolitical risk has become an essential skill for businesses.

**Specific projection for 2026:**

Looking ahead to that timeframe, several key dynamics will need to be monitored. The nature of the conflict in Ukraine will remain the most critical variable. If a freeze in the conflict takes hold, **2026 will mark the beginning of a partial and highly charged reconstruction of Ukraine** , with pilot projects financed by the initial profits from Russian assets, but with persistent reluctance from private investors to commit on a large scale.

For **Russia** , its war economy, while effective in the short term, will show signs of structural exhaustion. The cannibalization of its civilian economy will be evident, with a visible degradation of infrastructure and non-defense-related public services. Its dependence on China will have increased further, making it vulnerable to fluctuations in the Chinese economy and to Beijing's demands.

In **Europe** , the industrial competitiveness crisis stemming from the loss of cheap Russian gas will remain the number one challenge. **2026 will likely see an intense debate on a new form of European interventionism** , potentially a sovereign wealth fund to rival the American IRA, financed by new common debt, which will reignite tensions between northern and southern member states.

In the **United States** , the impact of the massive investment plans of the IRA and the CHIPS Act will be fully visible, with a resurgence of manufacturing production in certain sectors. However, the budgetary cost of these policies and their inflationary impact will remain a hotly debated political issue, potentially exacerbated by the results of previous elections.

Finally, the most significant global tension in 2026 will be **the increasingly difficult interplay between the G7's "de- risking " agenda and the "multi-alignment" agenda of the Global South powers** . Friction will arise on issues of technology transfer, standards for the green transition, and access to critical raw materials, making every major international negotiation a test of strength between these competing worldviews.

In short, the world that emerged from the war in Ukraine is not simply a world that has changed. It has been fundamentally rewired . The circuits of finance, energy, and technology no longer follow paths of least economic resistance, but rather the fault lines of the new global geopolitical map. Understanding this new topography is no longer optional. It is the essential condition for navigating the murky and perilous waters of the 21st century.

# END

www.ingramcontent.com/pod-product-compliance
Lightning Source LLC
LaVergne TN
LVHW090430210926
848480LV00002B/767